In the Land
of Light

In the Land of Light

Israel, a Portrait of Its People

Photographs by Rodney Smith

With an Introduction
by Elie Wiesel

Houghton Mifflin Company
Boston · 1983

Library of Congress Cataloging in Publication Data

Smith, Rodney L.
    In the land of light.

    1. Israel—Description and travel—Views. I. Title.
DS108.5.S57   1983   779'.02'0924   83-6130
ISBN 0-395-34425-5

Printed in the United States of America

First edition

H   10 9 8 7 6 5 4 3 2 1

For my wife Mary-Kelly,
whom I adore,
who has given me her love,
lifting my soul so I could see.

Acknowledgments

Several years ago, I was invited by Teddy Kollek, the mayor of Jerusalem, to come to Israel as a guest of the Jerusalem Foundation. For three months, my family and I stayed at the apartment-studio complex at Mishkenot Sha'ananim ("Peaceful Dwelling"), which the foundation places at the disposal of visiting artists, musicians, and writers. I want to thank the Jerusalem Foundation for this great privilege.

I had the further good fortune to team up with Jonathan Broder of NBC radio and the *Chicago Tribune*. His affable spirit, his knowledge of the country, and his ability to speak Hebrew and Arabic fluently were invaluable assets.

I would like to thank three good friends: Michael Malone and Kristin Helmore, for their generous help in the preparation of the text of this book, and Nathan Garland, the book's designer, for his initial faith in my work and for his help with both selecting the photographs and determining their sequence.

Most important, I wish to acknowledge and thank my editor, Nan Talese, for her enduring support. Anyone who has struggled to bring a first book to light knows how special it is to find an editor who is steadfast through great difficulty and who perseveres with integrity and grace.

Lastly, I would like to thank all the people I photographed. In their faces I saw not only the life of their diverse and vital races, but the life, changeless and unconquerable, of the human race, of which we are all members.

Mishkenot Sha'ananim, Jerusalem

Introduction

These men forever tracked by sadness, where do they come from? Where are they going, these women whom sorrow has made beautiful and secretive? I study their faces and find in them the imprint of memory.

Weathered faces, fierce with luminous eyes and haunted gaze: in what land, on what road, have I seen them? Unmoving in time, they are watchful and guarded; they suffer without showing it. They tell a story — always the same — to an invisible, anguished audience.

Gathered together in this ancient land where the descendants of the prophets live side by side with the survivors of pogroms, these people have their own particular manner of listening and expressing themselves, of loving with a smile, and smiling in silence, of denying emptiness and solitude with a simple gesture, with a distant song that reverberates like the humming of night as dawn approaches.

I love them: it is impossible not to love them. The mystery that makes them fascinating is also our own. It is about the struggle that man, eternally in exile, is condemned to wage so as not to founder, not to go astray, not to become misled.

How do they manage to prevail? For in their own way we can

see that they do prevail. We need only examine the expression in their eyes to realize this. To sense the serenity they convey is enough to make us recognize our kinship with them.

They quest by questioning. They call out through recollection. They each are bound to an event, to an image that acquires meaning through themselves. And they are the link between the event and the meaning.

Somewhere, men massacred beneath a pure blue sky. Women debased by a familiar or alien aggressor. Children beaten down, crazed with hunger and fatigue . . .

These are the thoughts of the men and women in this book of overwhelming seriousness and beauty. These people invoke their tortured past not out of complacency, but from a concern to share it; not for attention, but modestly and in order to exorcise it.

Thus, thanks to them, we may learn that man has the power to disarm evil by delving more deeply into its effects; that the victim can transcend suffering by transforming it into a reason to hope. Look at them live and dream, in action and at rest. Look at them through the eyes of the child in you, and you will recognize their silence as well as their need to understand.

These bloody memories, in which horror is mixed with despair, they have carried with them, within them. And yet they succeed, not in expunging them — this they will never do — but rather in conferring upon them a meaning that is humanizing.

Christians, Moslems, and Jews, young and old, peaceful villagers and wary mountainfolk, brought together from the four corners of the earth, from all forms of exile — each in his or her own way shows that, as a way of being, resignation is only a form of degradation. Everyone in these pages has proved his or her courage, by overcoming doubt and temptation in order to sound for the world a clarion cry to faith.

These men and women, these boys and girls, thrust forward onto the stage of history — they are the ones who, without knowing it, provide us with the one human justification without which it would be impossible to raise ourselves above defeat and tears.

Let us look at them as they live: perhaps the light that is shed will enlighten us.

—Elie Wiesel

The Garden of Olives

He went up under the gray foliage
all gray and merging with the olive lands
and laid his forehead that was full of dust
deep in the dustiness of his hot hands.

After everything this. And this was the end.
Now I must go, while I am turning blind,
and why dost Thou so will, that I must say
Thou art, when I myself do no more find Thee.

I find Thee no more. Not within me, no.
Not in the others. Not within this rock.
I find Thee no more. I am alone.

I am alone with all mankind's grief,
which I through Thee to lighten undertook,
Thou who art not. O nameless shame . . .

Later it was said: an angel came—.

Why an angel? Alas it was the night
leafing indifferently among the trees.
The disciples stirred in their dreams.
Why an angel? Alas it was the night.

The night that came was no uncommon night;
hundreds like it go by.
Then dogs sleep, and then stones lie.
Alas a sad night, alas any night
that waits till it be morning once again.

For angels come not to such suppliants,
and nights do not round about such grow large.
Who lose themselves by all things are let go,
and they are abandoned of their fathers
and shut out of their mothers' womb.

—Rainer Maria Rilke

A few miles from the Lebanese border the ancient Druse village of Peki'in sits sheltered in the mountains of Galilee. The earth is lush, hilly, and luxuriant. Little has changed there over the last two thousand years. Most people in Peki'in are still shepherds or farmers. Old men still sit in the public square, and donkeys crowd past goats in the twisting streets.

With a journalist friend, I drove down a cool, narrow, winding street into the heart of the stone village, the central square. There, in a flour mill, partly hidden by morning shadows, Druse women dressed in deep black robes were kneeling, grinding flour for the day's bread. Their purpose, their posture, their style, depicted to me an elemental form of life: an intimation of the very essence of human existence.

I was exhilarated, and desperately felt the need to take their photograph, but the women refused, hiding their faces. My friend urged me to go ahead, but I couldn't do it without their permission. I tried for hours with the help of interpreters to win their agreement, but to no avail. I felt I was failing to capture—in a moment as fleeting as light—the photograph of a lifetime.

Dismally dejected, I slumped away from the flour mill. Not a hundred yards off, down a little side street, a Druse man was standing by his door. He graciously invited me inside to have tea, but it was now late afternoon and we had to leave. I took his photograph quickly, then forgot about it.

Twice more I returned from Jerusalem, hoping to photograph the women at the mill. In the square the old men of Peki'in sat over their coffee, playing their cutthroat, breakneck-speed games of *sheshbesh* (our backgammon). My mother was herself a ruthless backgammon player, and trained by her from childhood, I actually managed to win a game against a local champion. My victory delighted the Druse players no end, and I was asked with enthusiastic gestures to visit their homes.

But I never again saw the women at the mill nor the man who had given so freely what I had longed for from them. It was not until months later, after coming home and processing the film, that I realized the power I would find in the photograph. I had felt so much regret over what I had lost that day that I was blind to what I had so easily gained.

Druse man, Peki'in

Garage mechanic, Jerusalem

Arab men, Old City, Jerusalem

In the Judean desert between Jerusalem and Jericho, I visited a Bedouin
camp. As we approached, I was both excited and terrified, for it is impossible
to predict how Bedouins will respond to a stranger.

We were ushered into the men's tent. The flap closed behind us. It was
inexplicably cool inside and the air smelled strongly of cumin, sheepskin,
coffee, and tobacco. Around me, their legs crossed on worn rugs, their
elbows on cushions, sat half a dozen dark-skinned, earthen-faced men with
large mustaches. They wore gray robes with black belts. Kaffiyehs were
wound around their heads, and huge scimitars lay beside them. We drank
numerous cups of Turkish coffee as we tried to get permission to photograph
in the camp.

After hours of discussion, we received permission to photograph
the men. My interpreter cautioned me nervously that it was forbidden to
photograph women unveiled, but my desire to do so was enormous, and I
kept pleading for permission. They burst out angrily, "No! No! Forbidden!"
I made my translator persist. In a sudden reversal, one of the men said I
could take two photographs of one of his wives if I would pay for the
privilege. I had never paid for a photograph, but this time I agreed.

When the woman heard what her husband had done, she was furious at
him, and amused with me. Finally she ran out of invectives and slowly, quietly, unveiled herself to me. A window was opened, an intimacy revealed.
I took two photographs and stopped, exhausted.

Opposite and above: Bedouin woman, Judean desert

Barbershop window, Jerusalem

Bakery, Mahane Yehuda, Jerusalem

Butcher shop, Old City, Jerusalem

Jerusalem. Clockwise from top left: Synagogue, Bukharian quarter;
Synagogue, Mea She'arim; Moslem quarter; Bus, West Jerusalem

Franciscan priest, Garden of Gethsemane

Garden of Gethsemane

In Israel I heard hundreds of stories about death. Every family looks back down a road of history crowded with war, horror, and grief. Not only the Jews who survived the Holocaust, but also Greeks, Armenians, and Arabs—all can tell you of tragedy. There is a sadness in this land, audible in these stories and visible in almost every face. Here is one person's tale, no worse than many others.

An elderly Armenian told me that, as a young boy of five, he had lain dead for several days. At first I did not understand what he meant. Pointing to a depression in his forehead, he said that Turkish soldiers, riding through his village on horseback and brandishing long scimitars, had struck off his father's head and stabbed his mother to death before his eyes. They clubbed him on the head and then rode away. He lay unconscious for several days before awakening.

I can't imagine how this man must have felt as a child seeing his parents killed. Yet he, like so many others, was not bitter or angry but had remained gentle, kind, and decent. I don't know where the faith—the ability to persevere and flourish—comes from in life, but people here have it. They are survivors; they *will* endure.

Armenian seminarian, Armenian quarter, Jerusalem

Opposite and above: Easter service, Armenian church, Jerusalem

During the Armenian and Greek Orthodox Easter services I was struck by the symbolic use of light, and what it says about a people's character.

The Armenian Mass, for example, is as dark and somber as this pillaged people's sense of their past. The chapel remains mysteriously dark. A procession of monks in long dark robes moves up the nave, chanting plainsong and swinging censors, which perfume the air with swirling smoke. The only illumination comes from long shafts of light, slanting downward from the high windows like small spotlights on a tragic stage.

For the Greek Orthodox, however, light expands until it fills the space of worship. This process is most dramatic on Holy Saturday. It begins once the congregation assembles, when the doors to the outside world are locked. Each of the celebrants holds an unlighted candle. A taper burning beside Christ's tomb is passed from hand to hand, sharing its flame with the congregation, until the chapel is flooded with an intense, brilliant light. Everything is illuminated, as if, through this rite, all the darkness in the world were being driven out.

Opposite: After Easter service, Armenian church, Jerusalem
Above: Armenian priests, Easter, Jerusalem

When I first read Genesis as a young boy, I felt that the world God had created was not the same as the world I lived in. My world seemed to be filled with darkness, but the Garden of Eden was a place where light had revealed God's purpose.

It was light that provided understanding, growth, and sustenance. Without it, there was darkness, despair, and remorse. Adam's banishment shut him out from serenity and safety, and abandoned him to loneliness and also, perhaps, to the possibility of eventual growth and unity. But it was the light that gave Eden significance for me.

When I walk through the gates of a monastery, I feel as if I am walking into that well-lit place. It is not the monks themselves who inspire this feeling in me; rather, it is the place they have created. The walls, the gardens, the trees, constitute a world that is uncluttered and serene. Its isolation from the world outside attracts me, yet it is the world outside the garden in which I live and love.

The Franciscan monastery of Latrun is unmistakably French. The bougainvillea, the lemon trees, the pastel pink walls with their Latin inscriptions, the winery and the gardens, made me feel I was somewhere in medieval Provence. Most of the monks had not left Latrun for many years, and the outside world was as foreign to them as Latrun was to me.

It took three visits before I got permission from the Father Superior to enter the inner quarters of the monastery, where the monks live and

Opposite and above: Latrun monastery

worship. When this finally had been arranged, I arrived early in the morning with my wife and three-year-old son, Jonah. It is forbidden for women to enter the monastery past the entryway, and Jonah, though allowed to go in with me, decided to stay with his mother.

As soon as I entered the large chapel from the outside gate, I felt the special quality of the place. The solitude appealed to me. Everything was proceeding at its own pace—slowly, methodically, and quietly. The monks, having taken vows of silence, did not speak; only my guide, a senior in his community, whispered to me softly. We left the chapel and proceeded deeper into the monastery, through the dormitories and finally into the library, each step a further transition from the public to a private, peaceful world.

Suddenly, from somewhere deep within the monastery, I heard a lonely, echoing cry: "Da–ddy! Da–ddy!"

My guide and I quickly retraced our steps to the large chapel we had first entered. Jonah had decided that he wanted to be with his father and had broken free of my wife and come to find me. Worse, Mary-Kelly, desperate to stop the noise, had chased after him and had timidly entered the chapel. Just at the moment she reached Jonah through one side door, we entered through another.

The senior monk's face was pale with incredulous shock: first, at the intrusion of a child searching for his father, and then at the transgression of the rule that no woman enter. Needless to say, we were banished.

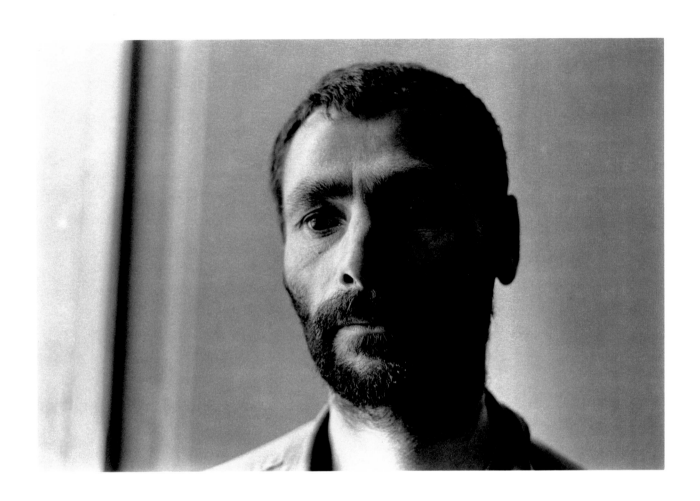

Franciscan monk, Latrun monastery

Opposite and above: Franciscan monk, Latrun monastery

Opposite and above: Latrun monastery

Holy Sepulchre compound, Jerusalem

Jewish quarter, Jerusalem

In the late afternoon of a warm spring day in Jerusalem, I was feeling happy and content. It was a few days before Passover, and I found myself in a very poor section of the city, which had been slated for demolition. Everything, however, had been freshly painted in white and pastels of pink and blue. Everyone was cleaning in preparation for the holiday.

In an obscure corner of this quarter I saw a window and doorway that intrigued me. I knew I wanted to photograph them, and I began to speak to the frail, elderly man inside, who, like all the others, was slowly and methodically sweeping out his tiny home.

He invited me in and, after working for some time, he stopped, quite exhausted, and sat down at his bare table to make tea. There was a lovely spareness and order to the room. The walls were whitewashed; there were a few simple wooden chairs, a table, and, in the corner, a spartan cot covered neatly with a gray blanket. The floor had a deep patina, and the window and doorway let afternoon light pour in.

We sat together, and he brought over a bowl with two apples in it, offering me one. It was not until later that I realized this was all he had to eat for the day. He graciously had given me, a stranger, half of his daily allotment.

After having met this man, I realized that the perspective was more appealing from the inside looking out than from the outside looking in.

Window, Jerusalem

Weeks before Easter, one could feel the anticipation building in Jerusalem. The Orthodox Easter falls on a different day from the Latin Easter, and as pilgrims from France and Germany were leaving, pilgrims from Greece, Cyprus, and Romania were beginning to pour in. It made Jerusalem even more eclectic than usual.

On the Greek Orthodox Good Friday I was up at dawn. Thousands of pilgrims had been quietly gathering in the city's holy places. So crowded and so restricted were the services that I never would have been able to attend the Good Friday Mass but for the intervention of the Greek Orthodox choirmaster. I had made friends with him some weeks before, and with wonderful good will he slipped me in among the choir. I found myself in the courtyard of the Church of the Holy Sepulchre, where I was overwhelmed to see thousands of pilgrims: a turbulent sea, mainly of Greek women dressed in black, grieving in prayer. The service was chanted in Greek by the Patriarch himself, and I was only a few feet away from him.

After the service was over, the women who had seen my proximity to the Patriarch desperately reached out to touch me. It was as if some of his holiness had been transferred to me, and that through me, they could be brought closer to the source of their salvation.

Greek Orthodox women, Good Friday, Church of the Holy Sepulchre, Jerusalem

Opposite and above: Good Friday, Church of the Holy Sepulchre, Jerusalem

Holy Week, Church of the Holy Sepulchre, Jerusalem

Jerusalem. Clockwise from top left:
Church of the Holy Sepulchre; Armenian priest;
Greek Orthodox priest; Armenian priest

Yemenite girl, Rosh Ha'ayin

Hasidic boy, Mea She'arim

Bedouin children, Judean desert

Perched on the roof of the Church of the Holy Sepulchre in Jerusalem is an Ethiopian sanctuary. As you climb the stairs from the turmoil of the Old City, you ascend into the tranquillity of a small African village, with shade trees and brightly whitewashed huts. Like its tall, graceful inhabitants, the presence of this quarter in the heart of the city is quiet and restrained.

When the Church of the Holy Sepulchre was built by the Crusaders over the supposed spot where Jesus was crucified and laid to rest on Calvary, all the Christian churches vied to establish themselves there. It is easy to understand how important it has been, through the centuries, for each Christian sect to call this supremely holy spot its own. Standing on the site of Calvary's drama, I too felt the holiness of this place: for so many, what happened there has made a difference for all time.

The Greek Orthodox, the Franciscans, the Armenians, the Copts, the Syrians, the Ethiopians, the Russian Orthodox, all have staked their claims to worship there. In the nineteenth century, the ruling Turks established a separate area for each denomination, based primarily on their size and power. Yet even today, two or more services are often held simultaneously, and the church rings with the sounds of the sects noisily trying to outsing each other.

When this partition occurred, the humble Ethiopians were banished to the roof, and built their village and chapel near the dome of the Holy Sepulchre. But if you look down through the windows in the dome, you notice that you are directly over Christ's tomb. By being relegated to the roof, the gentle Ethiopians have risen closer to the object of their devotion.

Opposite and above: Monk, Ethiopian monastery, Jerusalem

Woman, Ethiopian monastery, Jerusalem

Dome with two figures, Ethiopian monastery, Jerusalem

Woman, Ethiopian monastery, Jerusalem

Unlike the rolling hills of the Judean desert or the flat sweep of the Negev, the Sinai desert is jagged with mountains almost to the edge of the sea. The Sinai seems mysterious: neither Asian nor African, but something unique. The land is harsh, unchanging, primordial. For me, the mountains, the occasional thorn tree, the light, all speak of endurance and purity.

Thorn tree, Sinai

Shepherds. Top left and bottom right: In the Judean desert
Top right and bottom left: Near Latrun monastery

Bedouin woman with camel, Sinai

Deep within the cliffs of the valley of Kidron is the Greek Orthodox monastery of Mar-Saba, whose remoteness is intensified by the approach to it—a path through the Judean desert. As I drove farther away from Jerusalem into the desert, the mountains all around, the bleakness of the landscape, and the absolute quiet of the surrounding country made me feel cut off from the world.

Mar-Saba's thirty-foot walls seem to grow naturally out of the jagged landscape, and the ancient sandstone makes even more dazzling the intense blue of the monastery's medieval doorway. Within the fortress walls, this same blue trims the doorways and windows. I have seen this primary blue bordering the doors and windows of peoples as disparate as Arabs, Greeks, and the blacks who live on the Sea Islands of South Carolina. For some, the color magically averts the evil eye; for others, it serves as a barrier between external and internal, between sky and soul.

After gaining access to the monastery, I was led by one of the monks into Mar-Saba's chapel. Smoky with incense and aglitter with icons, it was as dark as the courtyard was luminous.

The twenty or so elderly monks at Mar-Saba are as diverse in origin as the crew of the *Pequod* in *Moby Dick*. I saw Turks, Chinese, Africans, and Greeks, all with long gray beards and clad in black robes, and all sent from their homes to this remote stronghold. Just before I left, one monk led me into a cavelike room, lit only by candlelight, where the skulls of monks who had lived and died at Mar-Saba over the centuries were piled against the walls in a macabre *memento mori*. Death's presence and smell were overwhelming. I wanted to leave, but also to stay. I felt that I had momentarily discovered some mysterious, frightening, and exhilarating truth.

Opposite: Monk, Mar-Saba monastery
Above: Interior, Mar-Saba monastery

Monk, Mar-Saba monastery

Monk, Mar-Saba monastery

Last Supper window, Old City, Jerusalem

Armenian church, Armenian quarter, Jerusalem

Man, Jaffa

Arab woman baking bread, Jish

Man, Mahane Yehuda, Jerusalem

Porter, Old City, Jerusalem

Sudanese shepherd, Jericho

Bedouin, Judean desert

Bedouins, Negev desert

Clockwise from top left: Arab man, Beit Jalla; Bedouin sheik,
Negev desert; Druse man, Peki'in; Bedouin, Negev desert

During my three months' stay in Wales, only once did someone refuse me permission to take his photograph. In the Middle East, almost everybody says no. At first.

Their professed reasons are various cultural, ethical, and religious rules: an Arab woman must not allow any man but her husband to see her face; an Orthodox Jew must create no graven image—which some believe includes photographs. Nevertheless, my experience was that for most, as for people everywhere, a fear of being thought ugly, and a reluctance to expose their imperfections, lay at the root of their refusals. Time and again when I persevered, and, in an effort to convince them of my respect, revealed myself, an adamant *no* would turn suddenly into a yes. This was particularly true if I could speak with the person alone, away from the pressures of pride, shyness, or embarrassment that force groups to a collective denial.

In Mea She'arim, the Hasidic quarter of Jerusalem, I visited a synagogue day after day in hopes of taking a photograph. After the punishing sun of the city streets, the dark stones and quiet voices within this synagogue were like an umbrella of tranquillity, sheltering worshipers who spend seven, eight, or nine hours a day studying the Talmud.

The first time I entered the synagogue, the congregation hurried me back outside, where everyone began yelling and screaming. Some shouted, "Forbidden!" but others told me, "Go ahead, take the picture!" One man tried to rip the camera off my neck; another put his arm around me affectionately. Finally, by the third or fourth visit, my persistence had won me a few more allies, but still not a photograph.

Then one morning when I came back, the light was extraordinary, and I asked permission to photograph in the room. Miraculously, everyone said, "Go right ahead." After all the squabbling and pleading of the past days, this moment arrived with a quiet ease.

Synagogue, Mea She'arim, Jerusalem

Hasidic Jews, Mea She'arim, Jerusalem

Hasidic Jews, Jerusalem. Clockwise from top left: Mahane Yehuda; Synagogue,
Bukharian quarter; Mea She'arim; Religious court, Mea She'arim

There is something about photographing old people at the edge of their lives
that has always appealed to me. I want to take care of them, cradle them,
listen to their stories, and laugh with them.

I am particularly attracted to those people who, I feel, have had a life of
hardship and yet, at the end of their lives, are ready to accept death—not
with resignation but forthrightly, with faith. Israel was full of people
like this: people whose lives could not have been more tortured, who had
witnessed brutality everywhere. Yet I felt often, particularly with old people,
a kind of gentleness, a peace.

Man, old-age home, Bukharian quarter, Jerusalem

Opposite and above: Man, old-age home, Bukharian quarter, Jerusalem

Man, old-age home, Bukharian quarter, Jerusalem

Woman, old-age home, Bukharian quarter, Jerusalem

Clockwise from top left: Man, Jerusalem; Hasidic Jew,
Jerusalem; Employee in a winery, Motza; Vintner, Motza

Man, Jerusalem

Garden, West Bank

Russian nunnery, Ein Kerem

Nun at pump, Russian nunnery, Ein Kerem

Landscape, Rosh Pina

Clockwise from top left: Olive grove, West Bank; Carpenter's shop,
Jerusalem; Stone house, Peki'in; Interior, Jerusalem

Clockwise from top left: Woman, Jerusalem; Bedouin woman, Negev;
Man in window, Jerusalem; Russian nun, Ein Kerem

Yemen is the underbelly of Saudi Arabia. Jews born there have an Arabic look and sensibility, but as Jews they were routinely persecuted in their homeland, forcing them to flee to Israel. Nevertheless, I found them a wonderfully sweet, easygoing, good-willed people.

What most delights me about this photograph is that none of the three people in it was aware of the presence of the other two.

Three Yemenites, Rosh Ha'ayin

Clockwise from top left: Man, outskirts of Jerusalem;
Street, Peki'in; Man, Rosh Ha'ayin; Man, Peki'in

Clockwise from top left: Arab, West Bank; Woman, synagogue, Jerusalem;
Druse man, Peki'in; Woman, camel market, Beer Sheba

Clockwise from top left: Synagogue, Bukharian quarter, Jerusalem;
Beggar, Old City, Jerusalem; Yemenites, Rosh Ha'ayin; Bedouins, Negev

Clockwise from top left: Independence Day celebration, Jerusalem;
Two men, Tel Aviv; Two children, Peki'in; Two men, Tel Aviv

Greek Orthodox Easter pilgrims, Jerusalem

Man, Rosh Ha'ayin

Clockwise from top left: Old-age home, Bukharian quarter, Jerusalem;
Hasidic man, synagogue, Mea She'arim; Easter pilgrims, Church of the
Holy Sepulchre, Jerusalem; Yemenite, synagogue, Rosh Ha'ayin

Clockwise from top left: Arab cemetery, Old City, Jerusalem;
Greek Orthodox priest, Easter services, Jerusalem; Catholic pilgrims,
Easter services, Jerusalem; Yemenites, Rosh Ha'ayin

Clockwise from top left: Man, Motza; Guard at the Church of the Holy Sepulchre, Jerusalem; Parsley vendor, Mahane Yehuda; Man, Tel Aviv

Clockwise from top left: Woman, Jerusalem; Woman, Peki'in;
Woman, Yemin Moshe, Jerusalem; Woman, Nuweiba, Sinai

Dome of the Rock, Jerusalem

Dome of the Rock, Jerusalem

Afterword

It is by the bow of a man's back, the way a woman moves her body, holds a cup, looks at me, by the way people dance and sing and laugh, that I understand them. I have a passion to get below the surface of things, to find an enduring essence. I want each of my photographs to express the underlying forces in life, each frame to be able to stand on its own. When a photograph succeeds for me, I feel that every inch of space is necessary. For these reasons, although I may spend hours in a place, I often shoot very little film.

I find I am always drawn to a subject: I may see something far away that excites me, even if it is only a sense of light or space. I run directly toward it and look through the viewfinder. I move closer or farther away in order to harmonize my relationship to the subject and to what I feel.

My passion for clarity is particularly manifest in the way I use a camera. Many photographers feel that, because the world is unclear, they have no obligation to make their photographs sharp. I agree that the world is unclear. Yet it is my compulsion to make the world as sharp as possible. By doing so, I try to expose more than is readily apparent. Thus I have some means of controlling chaos, if only by describing it. However, the acuity of a photograph does not always define life for me; detail sometimes reveals mystery.

I have spent years studying the technique of photography in search of a means to make a small-format 35-mm camera achieve the technical clarity of a large-format camera. I am never satisfied with the results of my work: the detail is never sharp enough; the light is never articulate enough. Though I marvel at the mastery of some large-format photographers, only the unobtrusiveness, speed, and agility of a 35-mm camera can achieve the closeness and intimacy I require in my portraits.

For me, the interaction between the photographer and the subject is crucial. In Israel, I often saw photographers cope with the difficulties of portraying people by standing at a distance and using a long-focal-length

123

lens. I want a person to be aware of me, to deal with my presence, and am therefore always physically close to the person I photograph. For these reasons I use only a normal-focal-length lens.

There is something about being face to face with someone that is necessary for my life. There is much in the world that terrifies me, so I need to get close to people—to reach out.

When I feel I am close I get closer: to remove everything from the frame that is extraneous and to scale down the photograph in hopes of achieving a simplicity that reveals only what I feel is in that person. I am so close that I cannot look the other way or hide behind anything. Then I am aware of an intensity of intimacy and understanding. I begin to sense who I am, and to perceive in others the small expressions that help to reveal a person's unique and essential quality.

People give a great deal to me. They trust me even though I am a stranger. I love them for their strength and for their willingness to reveal themselves to me face to face.

Easter pilgrims, Greek Orthodox compound, Jerusalem

In the Land of Light
was designed by Nathan Garland
of New Haven, Connecticut.

The text was set in Walbaum,
a classic early-nineteenth-century typeface,
produced in the style of Didot and Bodoni.
The photographs were reproduced
in laser-scanned, 300-line-screen duotones
by the Acme Printing Company
of Medford, Massachusetts,
on Cameo dull 80 lb. text paper made
by the S. D. Warren Company.
The book was bound by A. Horowitz and Son,
with cover cloth made
by The Holliston Mills.

The original photographs were printed
on Seagull paper supplied
by the Oriental Photo Distributing Company.